Lovingly Presented

To _____

From _Great Grandma_

On _Vi_

"Jesus loves the little children."

Dedicated to my dear friend, Dotty Thur,
lover of children and champion of
the true meaning of Christmas.

With special appreciation to Earle Fitz; the real-life
teacher of Page 74, whose early vision — thronged
with adventures — today stands as Riverside-World
Bible Publishers. His famous motto of "Service,
Service, Service!" flows from the heart of a man
whose hopes now bless children around the world.

Published by
WORLD BIBLE PUBLISHERS, INC.
Iowa Falls, Iowa

CHRISTIAN MOTHER GOOSE®

Rock-A-Bye Christmas

Selected Scripture from
The Authorized King James Version

Written and Illustrated
by
Marjorie Ainsborough Decker

CHRISTMAS THOUGHTS
from
CHRISTIAN MOTHER GOOSE

Christmas! The gentle magnet that draws kindness from our hearts; goodwill to all men; turns our thoughts to home — and reaches for the hands of little children.

It is their season! — their time! And a time of childlike wonder for all of us to behold the love and majesty of God's beautiful Gift, The Lord Jesus Christ.

May the pages of this little book be a light to the Father's house — to Jesus! — the heart, hope and heavenly calling of all Christmases past, and all the Christmases there ever shall be.

Marjorie Ainsborough Decker

LITTLE SHEM
OF BETHLEHEM

A long time ago,
   In the town of Bethlehem,
There lived a boy shepherd.
   They called him Little Shem.
His flock was just three sheep,
That he watched with loving care;
Leading them and feeding them
   On green grass here and there.

One night he brought them into town,
    To rest beside a stable.
They snuggled close around his knees,
    As close as they were able.
Then soon, the boy and tired sheep
    Fell fast asleep together,
Huddled in a mound of hay,
    Protected from the weather.

Sleeping fast, they didn't see
    A Baby born close by.
They didn't see the angels
    Who were singing in the sky.
They didn't see the shepherds,
    Who came from the hills to tell
That Jesus was that tiny Babe —
    The Lord Emmanuel!

But when they woke, a shining light
    Filled Little Shem with joy!
The Baby's mother smiled and said,
    "Come close, dear shepherd boy.
For little children all should come
    To God's dear, precious Son.
He loves them all and gave
    His Gift of Love for every one.

His Gift is in the manger —
  The Child from Heaven, Who came
To save us and to keep us;
  Jesus is His lovely Name."
The little shepherd touched the Babe,
  And Baby Jesus smiled,
For here on earth He had been given
  The love of this first child.

  And evermore in Bethlehem,
  Jesus was loved by Little Shem.

HAPPY BIRTHDAY!

Happy Birthday, dear Lord Jesus,
Thank You for this day we share;
Thank You for the love and goodness
On Your Birthday, everywhere.

*Let us be glad and rejoice, and
give honor to Him.*   Rev. 19:7

Jesus loves the little children,

Every little girl and boy.

So He came to earth to bring them

Unto God's great heart of joy.

Skip and dance! for He's the reason
We rejoice
This Christmas Season!

LITTLE CHRIST JESUS IS BORN!

Little Christ Jesus
is born, is born!
Little Christ Jesus is born!
With hands, feet and face
Like the children He made;
This is God's Son,
Bring the bugle brigade!
Heaven has come!
Blow trumpet and horn . . .
Little Christ Jesus
is born, is born!

. . . the Father sent the Son to
be the Savior of the world.
I John 4:14

10

Dear Lord,
I am a little boy,
And I would like to say,
All little boys like gifts
That they can build,
And fly and play.
If three wise boys
Had seen the star
That led to Jesus' side,
We would have brought Him
Puzzles, games,
And kites to fly and glide.

Thank You for listening,
Amen.

UNDERNEATH THE MANGER

Mrs. Mollybeth Mouse
　　Was looking for
　　　A warm, new house.
She crept into a stable
　　Underneath a bed of straw.
And there she made a house,
　　Nice and cozy for a mouse,
With a handy little hole,
　　That was really her front door.

Through the door she took a peep
　　At a donkey and some sheep,
As she heard a gentle voice say,
　　"Lay Jesus on the straw.
The cattle in the stall,
　　And the little creatures small,
Will be welcome here to sleep
　　Round the manger, on the floor."

Mrs. Mollybeth Mouse
    Looked around her warm, new house,
It was filled with shining light,
    Much more beautiful than gold!
For the Savior laid His head
    On the manger for His bed,
Where a little mouse stayed warm
    Underneath Him from the cold.

*The Lord is good to all: and
His tender mercies are over all
His works.*   Psalm 145:9

THE CALENDAR OF MY HEART

The calendar says
It's Christmas!
It marks the day
It will start.
But, Christmas Day
Is every day
In the calendar
Of my heart.

*This is the day which the Lord
hath made.* Psalm 118:24

HUMPTY DUMPTY'S CHRISTMAS SONG

Humpty Dumpty sat on a wall,
  Humpty Dumpty had a great fall;
Humpty Dumpty shouted, "Amen!
  God can put me together again."

Christmas brings us all together,
  'Cross the miles and 'cross the sea;
May God bring you all together
  In one happy family.

MY CHRISTMAS PRAYER

Dear Father up in Heaven,
　　I pray this Christmas prayer,
For all who feel so lonely,
　　And who have no one to care.
I pray You'll send an angel —
　　Well — I mean a Mom or Dad,
To bring them home for Christmas,
　　Where their Christmas will be glad.

*Inasmuch as ye have done it
unto one of the least of these
my brethren, ye have done it
unto me.* 　 Matt. 25:40

TWINKLE, TWINKLE,
CHRISTMAS STAR

Twinkle, twinkle, little star,
God has placed you
where you are,
Up above the world so high,
You're God's light hung in the sky.

Twinkle, twinkle, Christmas Star,
Bringing wise men from afar;
Guiding them to God's Dear Son
Who lights the Way for all to come.

CHRISTIAN MOTHER GOOSE'S
Christmas Card

All over the town,
    From streets and from steeple,
From houses and hills,
From all kinds of people,
The story is told
Of that first Christmas when
Love came from Heaven,
As the Savior of men.
Over and over,
It is told with delight;
Here is the story
Of that glorious night . . .

And there were in the same country shepherds abiding in the field, keeping watch over their flock by night.

And, lo, the angel of the Lord came upon them, and the glory of the Lord shone round about them: and they were sore afraid.

And the angel said unto them, Fear not: for, behold, I bring you good tidings of great joy, which shall be to all people.

For unto you is born this day in the city of David a Savior, which is Christ the Lord.

And this shall be a sign unto you; Ye shall find the babe wrapped in swaddling clothes, lying in a manger.

—Luke 2:8-18

WHITE SNOW, WHITE SNOW

White snow, white snow,
  Softly floating down.
White snow, white snow,
  Covering all the town.
Sent from Heaven to show us
  The message of God's love;
Turning everything to white
  From far, far above.

  Do you know the message
  Of the soft, white snow?
  God wrote it in the Bible,
  Long, long ago.

THREE KIND MICE,
ONE CHRISTMAS EVE

Three Kind Mice, one Christmas Eve,
  Looked at the falling snow,
With their noses pressed against the pane
  Of a Christmas window's glow.
Their fire was warm and cozy;
  They were glad to be inside;
When, out there in the moonlit night,
  A little mouse they spied.

The shivering, little creature
    Trudged along a snowy mound,
Gathering wood and bits of twigs
    That had fallen on the ground.
He didn't have a coat,
    And he didn't have a hat.
Said three Kind Mice, together,
    "Oh! we must take care of that!"

They wrapped up roasted nuts,
    Tied up logs, and cheese and bread;
Then found a woolly coat,
    And a hat of Christmas red.
"And now, a special present
    We must take, as well," they said.
"A flute and game we'll give him;
    Off we go! full steam ahead."

So, off into the cold
    Three Kind Mice went, one by one.
Following the footprints
    Where the poor, cold mouse had gone.
At last they reached a tree-trunk,
    And they tapped upon the door.
It opened up so slowly
    By the mouse they'd seen before.

He could not believe his eyes,
  At the sight of Three Kind Mice,
Loaded down with wood, and bags
  Of things that smelled so nice.
"May we come in and light a fire?
  Good friend, this Christmas Eve.
You'll give us joy tonight
  If our gifts you will receive."

Quite soon, the fire was crackling,
  As the cheese and nuts were spread.
The little mouse tried on his coat,
  And the hat of Christmas red.
"The clothes fit very nicely;
  Thank you all, oh! thanks," he said.
Then all four mice sat down to munch
  The cheese and crusty bread.

The tree-trunk house glowed brightly
  With the laughter of each mouse;
Oh! what a happy Christmas Eve
  Of games inside that house!
"My home will never be the same,
  How can I thank you friends,"
The little mouse said wistfully,
  As the evening reached its end.

"Well, someday *you* will help someone,
  And that is 'thanks', indeed.
That's how we pass our thanks along,
  With every good, kind deed."
The Three Kind Mice stepped out again
  In snowy, cold moonlight.
"Merry Christmas! little friend,"
  They cried, with their "Goodnight."

And as they braved the frosty air,
  With twinkling stars about,
They sang their favorite Christmas song:
  "Good King Wenceslas looked out . . ."

LITTLE BOY BLUE'S CAROL

Little Boy Blue
    Come, blow your horn,
The sheep's in the stable
    Where The Savior is born.
Where is the boy
    Who looks after the sheep?
Watching Baby Jesus,
    Fast asleep.

Dear Baby Jesus
I know you are King;
I bring a carol
For children to sing:
"If in a palace
You had to be born,
I could not stand
By Your side
With my horn.

But in a manger
In Bethlehem town,
Shepherds and children
May come to bow down;
Shepherds and children
May come to bow down."

*The shepherds returned,
glorifying and praising God for
all the things that they had heard
and seen . . . Luke 2:20*

HICKORY, DICKORY, DOCK

Hickory, dickory, dock,
   Dear Mouse,
Stay out of my sock!
All the treats
I will share,
If you'll not
Nibble there,
Hickory, dickory, dock.

⚜ CHARLIE CRICKET'S ⚜
MERRY MAILBAG

Oh! what a happy time it is;
 It's the best time of the year,
When a mailman's bag
 Is filled with cards
Of blessings and good cheer!
 Oh! merry mailman! merry bag!
Merry homes on which I call.
 From Charlie Cricket's merry mail —
Merry Christmas, one and all!

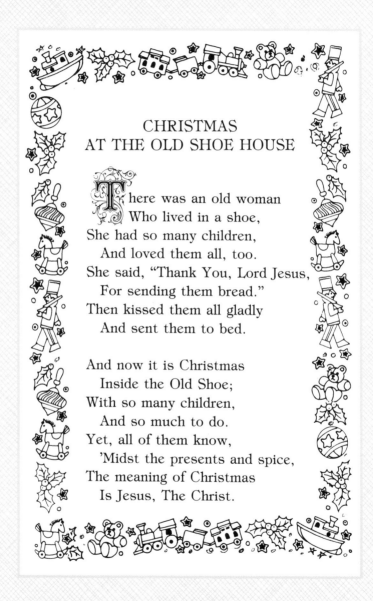

CHRISTMAS
AT THE OLD SHOE HOUSE

There was an old woman
Who lived in a shoe,
She had so many children,
And loved them all, too.
She said, "Thank You, Lord Jesus,
For sending them bread."
Then kissed them all gladly
And sent them to bed.

And now it is Christmas
Inside the Old Shoe;
With so many children,
And so much to do.
Yet, all of them know,
'Midst the presents and spice,
The meaning of Christmas
Is Jesus, The Christ.

In this was manifested the love of God toward us, that God sent His only begotten Son into the world, that we might live through Him. I John 4:9

～ THE ONE! ～

JESUS!
   The One Who fed five thousand
   With a young boy's fish and bread.
JESUS!
   The One Who calmed the storm
   With a few words that He said.
JESUS!
   The One Who healed the sick,
   And Who made the blind to see.
JESUS!
   The One Who loves each child,
   And Who blessed them on His knee.
JESUS!
   The One Who died and rose
   As the Savior of all men.
JESUS!
   The One Who once was born
   A little Child in Bethlehem.

That signs and wonders may be
done by the Name of thy holy
child Jesus.   Acts 4:30

LITTLE VISITOR

I wish I could have touched
The Baby Jesus in the stall,
And held His little hand —
Without squeezing tight, at all.
I know He would have smiled,
Being glad to see me there;
But I am glad today
That I can visit Him in prayer.

⟶❆ I LOVE THE SMELLS ❆⟵
OF CHRISTMAS

I love the smells of Christmas;
  Plum pudding, gingerbread;
The pine tree, Christmas cookies;
  Spicy apple-butter spread.
I love the little baskets,
  Filled up so we can take
Mother's treats to older friends,
  Who can no longer bake.
I thank You, dearest Jesus,
  For coming down to earth,
And for these happy Christmas smells
  That praise Your day of birth.

OVER THE HILL

Over the hill go Jack and Jill,
  And through the fields below;
Riding behind a jolly horse,
  In a sleigh, through frosty snow.
Goosey Gander has stopped his flight,
  To hear them as they sing:
"Joy to all the world tonight,
  Let earth receive her King."

And she brought forth her firstborn son, and wrapped him in swaddling clothes, and laid him in a manger; because there was no room for them in the inn.
Luke 2:7

NO ROOM

Dearest friend, Lord Jesus,
If I'd been in that Inn,
I'd have given You my room
To sleep Your first days in.
It makes me feel so sad
That You could only find a stall,
When You came here to make a room
In Heaven for us all.

I KNOW

I know
that God loves Christmas,
And I know He loves me, too,
Because He wrapped up Jesus
For His Gift to me and you.

Thanks be unto God for
His unspeakable Gift.
II Cor. 9:15

CHRISTMAS AT THE NOOKS AND CRANNIES

Christmas is coming
    To the Nooks and Crannies,
To each cozy home
    Of the Gramps and Grannies.
Instead of Christmas cards,
    Gramps and Grannies bake rolls,
Then stuff them with verses
    On wee, paper scrolls.
    Some say, "He is born!
    Come, worship The King!"
    Some say, "Peace, Goodwill,
    Good Tidings I bring."
    Some say, "Christ, The Lord
    In Bethlehem lay."
    Some say, "Praise The Lord!
    For this is His day."

Then off through the snow,
    With their wagon of rolls,
    Gramps and Grannies all go —
    Joyful, good-hearted souls!
Giving rolls all around,
    With a song of good cheer:
"We wish you a Merry Christmas,
    And a happy New Year!"

Rejoice in the Lord alway; and
again I say, Rejoice. Phil. 4:4

CHRISTMAS IS COMING!

Christmas is coming!
Let's open up God's Book.
Let's read the Christmas story;
I know just where to look.
Saint Luke and Saint Matthew,
Let's read them once again;
The story of dear Jesus
As a Babe in Bethlehem.

Now when Jesus was born in
Bethlehem of Judaea in the days
of Herod the king, behold, there came
wise men from the east to Jerusalem,
Saying, Where is he that is born
King of the Jews? for we have seen
his star in the east and are come to
worship him.

And, lo, the star, which they saw in the east, went before them, till it came and stood over where the young child was.

When they saw the star, they rejoiced with exceeding great joy.

And when they were come into the house, they saw the young child with Mary his mother, and fell down, and worshiped him: and when they had opened their treasures, they presented unto him gifts; gold, and frankincense, and myrrh.

—*Mat. 2:1,2,9-11*

HOW DANNY DORMOUSE
FOUND CHRISTMAS

Danny Dormouse
   Belonged, they say,
To a family who liked to work and play
   For only eight months of each year;
The other months, they'd disappear.
   As soon as winter came around,
The Dormouse family went underground.
   Burrowing in their hide-away,
They said, "Goodnight,
   Next spring we'll play."
Closed their eyes; snored once or twice;
   Then slept all winter — silent mice.
So, Christmas they had never kept;
   They missed it all; they slept and slept.
         Until . . .

Danny Dormouse, one November,
   Strayed too far and couldn't remember
The way back to the oak-tree mound,
   Where his family wintered underground.
He roamed and looked, with trembling chin,
   For someone who would take him in.
At last he saw a sign that read:
"Daddy Badger's Old Homestead."

Tired and hungry, and quite footsore,
  Danny tapped gently on the door.
Old Daddy Badger saw his plight:
  "Welcome, you can stay each night.
Through the winter we can talk and chat;
  Play games, tell tales,
And things like that."

Days passed, and just for friendship's sake,
    Danny tried hard to stay awake,
But kept on dozing by candlelight,
    Till Old Daddy Badger said, one night,
"Tonight is Christmas Eve, and when
    The kindest deeds are done by men.
We'll make our way, and quietly creep
Into a home where children sleep.

So, out the door and close together,
    They scampered off in winter's weather.
The cold made Danny blink his eyes.
    He was wide awake, to his surprise!
"Get ready!" Daddy Badger said,
    "For while your family sleeps in bed,
The sights inside this nearby house
    Haven't been seen by *any* Dormouse!"

And what did Danny see?...

A Christmas tree with lights aglow;
   Cakes and cookies, row upon row.
Boxes with ribbons tied and curled;
   Sweet music playing, "Joy to the world!"
A table set with tasty treats;
   The badger whispered, "Let's not eat.
This is the time of all goodwill;
   We'll wait till the children
Have their fill."

Creeping through the manger's straw,
    They tip-toed quietly out the door.
Out in the cold, not making a sound,
    Into the woods, past an oak-tree mound.
Danny cried out with a squeaky cheer,
"This is my home! I'm home, stop here!"

    "Home for Christmas,"
        Daddy Badger smiled,
    "The right place
        For every creature's child."
    Danny smiled, too,
        "Oh, thank you, friend,
    I'll be off to sleep
        Till winter's end.
    When the rest wake up,
        Will they believe
    I have seen all the wonders
        Of Christmas Eve?"

Well . . . the Dormouse family did!

REMEMBERING

Christmas is such
An exciting day,
I must remember
To thank God and pray:
"Thank You for Jesus,
And all things so glad;
And thank you for my
Dear Mommy and Dad."

Bethlehem . . . though thou be little . . . yet out of thee shall He come forth unto me.
Micah 5:2

MY BETHLEHEM

Oh, little town of Bethlehem,
  A tiny town on earth,
God chose you as the special place
  For our dear Savior's birth.
And God has chosen me, a child,
  Though little I may be,
For our dear Savior to come in
  And live His life through me.

49

PRAISE HIM, STILL!

Angels praised Him,
  In the sky;
Shepherds praised Him,
Standing by;
Wise men praised Him
When they came;
Mary praised
His lovely Name;
Joseph praised Him
In the stall;
Cattle praised Him,
Creatures all;
Children praised Him,
Where He lay.
Oh, praise Him, still!
This Christmas Day.

MERRY CHRISTMAS!

Merry Christmas! is the call,
"And God bless us, one and all!"
Hear it up and down the street;
Hear it from the friends you meet;
Hear it as the robins sing;
Hear it as the church bells ring;
Hear it in each happy hymn;
Hear it from dear Tiny Tim.
"Merry Christmas!" is the call,
"And God bless us, one and all!"

JEREMIAH OBADIAH'S TIDINGS

Jeremiah Obadiah
 Climbed the wall of Nehemiah.
With a trumpet in his hand,
He woke the folk across the land:
 "Christ is born!
 The shepherds tell
 They have seen Emmanuel!"
 Jeremiah Obadiah
 Called: "Come, worship
 Our Messiah!"

GRANDPA MOLE'S
Christmas Card

Merrily sails the Sharing Ship,
On Christmas Day
   in the morning.
Sailing off on a sharing trip,
On Christmas Day in the morning.
Filled with food and gifts to share,
At each village, here and there.
Merrily sails the Sharing Ship,
On Christmas Day in the morning.

53

WHEN MOTHER WAS VERY SMALL

When I was very, very small,
   Mother said to me,
"We threaded popcorn on a string,
To dress the Christmas tree.
We cut out snowflakes, lacy white,
And painted pine cones red;
Then hung them on the Christmas tree,
With men of gingerbread.
Dad carved a little manger scene;
I made the Christmas star;
And Grandma made the fruit and jam,
In dressed-up Christmas jars.
Our tree and presents were so grand,
They were the best of any!
And, do you know, they hardly cost
Us all a single penny!

Those were the days —
God bless them all!
When I was very, very small."

DOWN THE SIDE
OF CHRISTMAS HILL

What fun to ride a Christmas sled
Down the side of Christmas Hill!
The highest hill in all the town,
Where a Christmas star shines still.

Dashing, flashing,
Gliding, sliding,
Hoping I won't spill.
Whisking, frisking,
Quivering, shivering,
Laughing at the chill.
Rushing, brushing,
Bounding, rounding,
All the way downhill.
Bumping, jumping,
Rumbling, tumbling,
Humming, "Peace, Goodwill."

What fun to ride a Christmas sled
Down the side of Christmas Hill!

56

LITTLE MISS MUFFET'S
Christmas Card

Christmas prayer
   Fly here and there;
Peace and love
   With all to share.
Never stopping
   In your flight,
Bringing blessings
   Day and night;
Bringing joy
   And Christmas cheer
To our friends
   Throughout the year.

WISE MAN, WISE MAN

Wise man, wise man,
Did a wondrous star
Guide you and lead you
To Bethlehem afar?

Wise man, wise man,
Did you find a King?
A little Child
Without a crown,
You knelt a-worshiping?

Wise man, wise man,
Did you take Him gold?
Frankincense and myrrh?
Then return as you were told?

Wise child, wise child,
What you ask is true.
The Child, The King we worshiped,
Came from Heaven for me and you.

The Lord is my Shepherd;
I shall not want.
Psalm 23:1

LITTLE BO-PEEP'S CHRISTMAS CARD

Little Bo-Peep
Has lost her sheep
And doesn't know where
To find them;
But Jesus knows
And can bring them home,
Wagging their tails
Behind them.

All we like sheep
Have gone astray,
So Jesus came down
To find us.
He loves His sheep,
And will bring them home,
Let each Christmas Day
Remind us.

HEY, DIDDLE, DIDDLE

Hey, diddle, diddle,
   A rhyme and a riddle:
Why are the children
All yawning?
They couldn't sleep tight,
They kept waking all night,
For the clock to chime
Christmas dawning!

THE TWELVE DAYS
OF CHRISTMAS

On the first day of Christmas,
   In Christ's Nativity,
Is The Love Gift for you and me.

On the second day of Christmas,
   In Christ's Nativity:
   Joseph and Mary,
And The Love Gift for you and me.

On the third day of Christmas,
  In Christ's Nativity:
  Three Wise Men riding,
  Joseph and Mary,
And The Love Gift for you and me.

On the fourth day of Christmas,
  In Christ's Nativity:
  Four lambs a-hiding,
  Three Wise Men riding,
  Joseph and Mary,
And The Love Gift for you and me.

On the fifth day of Christmas,
  In Christ's Nativity:
  Five oxen grazing,
  Four lambs a-hiding,
  Three Wise Men riding,
  Joseph and Mary,
And The Love Gift for you and me.

On the sixth day of Christmas,
  In Christ's Nativity:
  Six sheep a-gazing,
  Five oxen grazing,
  Four lambs a-hiding,
  Three Wise Men riding,
  Joseph and Mary,
And The Love Gift for you and me.

On the seventh day of Christmas,
In Christ's Nativity:
Seven doves a coo-ing,
Six sheep a-gazing,
Five oxen grazing,
Four lambs a-hiding,
Three Wise Men riding,
Joseph and Mary,
And The Love Gift for you and me.

On the eighth day of Christmas,
In Christ's Nativity:
Eight cows a-mooing,
Seven doves a-cooing
Six sheep a-gazing
Five oxen grazing,
Four lambs a-hiding,
Three Wise Men riding,
Joseph and Mary,
And The Love Gift for you and me.

On the ninth day of Christmas,
    In Christ's Nativity:
    Nine hens a-laying,
    Eight cows a-mooing,
    Seven doves a-cooing,
    Six sheep a-gazing,
    Five oxen grazing,
    Four lambs a-hiding,
    Three Wise Men riding,
    Joseph and Mary,
And The Love Gift for you and me.

On the tenth day of Christmas,
   In Christ's Nativity:
   Ten Shepherds praying,
   Nine hens a-laying,
   Eight cows a-mooing,
   Seven doves a-cooing,
   Six sheep a-gazing,
   Five oxen grazing,
   Four lambs a-hiding,
   Three Wise Men riding,
   Joseph and Mary,
And The Love Gift for you and me.

On the eleventh day of Christmas,
   In Christ's Nativity:
   Eleven angels singing,
   Ten Shepherds praying,
   Nine hens a-laying,
   Eight cows a-mooing,
   Seven Doves a-cooing,
   Six sheep a-gazing,
   Five oxen grazing,
   Four lambs a-hiding,
   Three Wise Men riding,
   Joseph and Mary,
   And The Love Gift for you and me.

*The gift of God is eternal life
through Jesus Christ our Lord.*
Rom. 6:23

On the twelfth day of Christmas,
　In Christ's Nativity:
　Twelve bells a-ringing,
　Eleven angels singing,
　Ten Shepherds praying,
　Nine hens a-laying,
　Eight cows a-mooing,
　Seven doves a-cooing,
　Six sheep a-gazing,
　Five oxen grazing,
　Four lambs a-hiding,
　Three Wise Men riding,
　Joseph and Mary,
And The Love Gift for you and me.

MARY SAID

"What is His Name?"
   The stable boy asked.
"His Name is Jesus,"
   Mary said.
"Where is His home?"
   The stable boy asked.
"His home is Heaven,"
   Mary said.
"Why is He here?"
   The stable boy asked.
"He came to save us,"
   Mary said.
"Why will He save us?"
   The stable boy asked.
"Because He loves us,"
   Mary said.
"Where will He live?"
   The stable boy asked.
"He'll live in our hearts,"
   Mary said.

*For God so loved the world, that
he gave his only
begotten Son . . .* John 3:16

CLIPPETY-CLOP

Clippety-Clop, Clippety-Clop,
Carrying Baby Jesus home.
Back to Joseph's carpenter shop.
Clippety-Clop, Clippety-Clop.

Clippety-Clop, Clippety-Clop,
Joseph, Mary, Jesus and me.
Little brown donkey with Jesus atop,
Clippety-Clop, Clippety-Clop.

→ MR. BOBOLINK'S CAROL →

Cheery Mr. Bobolink,
   You're not very big —
A-singing and a-rocking
   On a little holly twig.
Do you know it's Christmas?
   And is your song, I pray,
A Bobolink's own carol
   Sung for Jesus on His day?

*Let everything that hath
breath praise the Lord.*
Psa. 150:6

DECEMBER
CAME A-CREEPING

December came a-creeping,
  Bringing bags of frost and ice;
Chasing boys and girls indoors,
  Along with cold field mice.

December came a-creeping,
  Pinching noses rosy-red;
Freezing toes and fingers;
  Prodding boys and girls to bed.

December came a-creeping,
  Thinking he had won his way;
But boys and girls braved all his tricks
  To go carolling Christmas Day.

THE TRUE MEANING OF CHRISTMAS

What is the meaning of Christmas?"
   A teacher asked his class,
In a small schoolhouse in the country,
   Nestled down in cornstalks and grass.

As quick as a wink, little Raymond
   Said, "Feasting with family and friends."
Dorothy raised her hand to say,
"But Santa Claus comes at the end."

Then Emery stood up to answer,
   With his shoulders true and straight,
"The meaning of Christmas is Christ;
   It's *His* birthday we celebrate."

The teacher looked at his students;
   Two out of three didn't know
The meaning of Christmas is Jesus,
   The Savior Who loves them all so.

Right here, the teacher decided
    He'd take Bibles across the land,
So that the true meaning of Christmas,
    Little children would understand.

Then, true to his promise and calling,
    He set off to fill the great need
Of planting Bibles everywhere,
    Like old Johnny Appleseed.

Today, you can't count all the children
    Who learned from the Bible story
The lovely true meaning of Christmas —
    Jesus Christ, The Lord of glory.

*For unto you is born this day in
the city of David a Savior,
which is Christ the Lord.*
Luke 2:11

HOLDING HEAVEN

Mary, you are holding Heaven,
Within your warm embrace.
How blessed you are
To be the first
To look on Jesus' face.
Wrap Him in your peasant shawl,
Hold Him close from harm;
The tiny Child
Who just before
Held earth within *His* arm!

*The eternal God is thy
refuge, and underneath are the
everlasting arms*...Deut. 33:27

THE FIRST CROWN

"Daughter, dear daughter,
 I've a story to tell,"
Said a Bethlehem shepherd
 To his child he loved well.
"God's angel came down
 In a glorious light,
As we simple shepherds
 Kept watch through the night."

"He said he had news
   Of great gladness and joy!
A Savior is born —
   Christ, The Lord — a Boy!
Then thousands of angels
   Appeared in a choir;
Heaven was opened
   To praise our Messiah!"

"But, wonder of wonders!
   I cannot tell all,
We found the wee King
   In a poor manger stall,
Wrapped up in swaddling clothes —
   This was the sign —
God's Son lay before us,
   God's Kingdom Divine!"

"Oh! father, dear father,"
   The little girl said,
"Then I'll make a little
   Green crown for His head!"
With tiny green leaves,
   And some blossoms of white,
She fashioned a crown
   In the morning's first light.

Then off to the manger
   The little girl sped;
The first crown for Jesus
   To place on His head.
With a little green crown —
   All the child could afford —
She crowned Baby Jesus
   Messiah and Lord!

DING, DONG, DELL

Ding, dong, dell,
　　Rings the Christmas bell.
Ding, dong, dell,
　　It's ringing out to tell:
Jesus, the Savior,
　　Was born this happy day;
Oh! come and join together
　　To worship Him and pray.
Ding, dong, dell,
　　Rings the Christmas bell.

THE LITTLE TREE'S WISH

Poor little tree, it had
   stood the whole year,
Empty of leaves,
With its branches all bare.
   "If I could be green
Like the pine tree," he spoke;
   "Or red like the maple;
Or gold like the oak.
   If I could be dressed
For one wonderful night,
   How happy I'd be
At the beautiful sight."

His dry, wrinkled branches
    Hung down to his side;
And there, all alone,
    The poor little tree cried.
But standing close by
    Was an angel who knew
What the little tree needed;
    He knew what to do.

And as the sun set
    On the poor little tree,
A cloud of soft snowflakes
    Danced down merrily.
Hour after hour
    They dressed him in white,
Then hung crystal jewels,
    To his great delight.

Bejeweled and crowned,
    Like a prince, royally,
The snow cloud dressed only
    The poor little tree.
The pine tree looked down
    At each silvery bough,
Then said to the maple,
    "He's beautiful now!"

The glad little tree
  Raised his branches on high,
And said to a star
  Twinkling up in the sky:
"This night is a miracle night,
  I believe!"
The angel then smiled. . .
  It was Christmas Eve!

⤙❧ MARY'S LULLABY ❧⤚

Rock-a-bye, rock-a-bye,
   Dear Baby, Gift of grace.
Rock-a-bye, rock-a-bye,
God's love shines from your face.
Rock-a-bye, rock-a-bye,
Sweet Baby Jesus, sleep.
My little Prince of Peace,
And The Shepherd of God's sheep.

For unto us a child is born,
unto us a son is given . . . and
His name shall be called The
Prince of Peace.   Isaiah 9:6

JOSEPH'S SONG

Along the road from Bethlehem,
Joseph sang a song
To little Baby Jesus
As they jiggety-jogged along:
  "I will teach you
  The carpenter's trade,
  Little Baby Jesus.
  Teach you how a yoke is made,
  Little Baby Jesus.
  Tables, chairs and farming plows;
  Games we'll make from olive boughs;
  I will teach you
  The carpenter's trade,
  Little Baby Jesus."

ROCK-A-BYE JESUS

Rock-a-bye, Jesus,
There on the hay.
Safely God brought You
To earth Christmas Day.
Little Lord Jesus
Wrapped up in the stall,
God will watch over
His Gift to us all.

Glory to God in the highest,
and on earth peace,
good will toward men.
Luke 2:14

CHRISTMAS STOCKINGS

What do you think of
The earth tonight?"
Asked an angel out in space,
To another angel looking down
At the earth's red-stockinged face.
"It's such a merry sight to see
The earthling sisters
And brothers,
Sharing gifts so happily,
Acting kindly one to another.
The Lord, Himself,
Must smile to see
The children's socks tick-tocking,
On His birthday merrily
Making miles of
Christmas stockings!"

BEAUTIFUL GIFT

Beautiful world,
Beautiful streams;
Beautiful sun,
Beautiful beams;
Beautiful stars,
Beautiful trees;
Beautiful gifts . . .
We thank God for these.
Beautiful Christ,
From Heaven above,
Beautiful Gift of
Beautiful Love.

*Behold, what manner of love
the Father hath bestowed
upon us . . . I John 3:1*

UP WHERE STARS
AND PLANETS FLY

Up where stars and planets fly,
   The angels rushed about the sky.
In and out the Milky Way,
   In such unheavenly disarray.
In joy, they shouted out in space,
   "He's born! The earth can see His face!"
And far, far, far, way down below,
   The little planet earth shone so,
In all the universe that night,
   There never was a brighter sight,
As, nestling in a bed of hay,
   The Savior brought us Christmas Day.

*In him was life; and the life was
the light of men.*   John 1:4

WAKE THEM!

The nightingale sang
  A royal song:
    Jesus is born! Jesus is born!
The rose wafted scent
  The whole night long:
    Jesus is born! Jesus is born!
The olive trees waved
  Their branches high:
    Jesus is born! Jesus is born!
The stars twinkled bright
  Against the sky:
    Jesus is born! Jesus is born!
The lambs bleated softly
  With the sheep:
    Jesus is born! Jesus is born!
But the rest of the world
  Lay fast asleep . . .
Oh, wake them! Wake them!
  Jesus is born!

WEE WILLIE WINKIE'S
Christmas Blessing

Wee Willie Winkie
Runs through the town,
In his Christmas stockings
And his nightgown;
Leaving Christmas letters
On each window-sill,
To bless the little children
With God's love and God's goodwill.

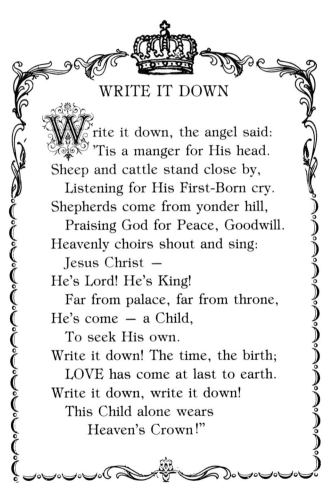

WRITE IT DOWN

Write it down, the angel said:
'Tis a manger for His head.
Sheep and cattle stand close by,
   Listening for His First-Born cry.
Shepherds come from yonder hill,
   Praising God for Peace, Goodwill.
Heavenly choirs shout and sing:
   Jesus Christ —
He's Lord! He's King!
   Far from palace, far from throne,
He's come — a Child,
   To seek His own.
Write it down! The time, the birth;
   LOVE has come at last to earth.
Write it down, write it down!
   This Child alone wears
      Heaven's Crown!"

*We see Jesus . . . crowned with
   glory and honor.*   Heb. 2:9

CHRISTMASTIME!

Christmastime!
It fills our hearts
With love and Christmas cheer;
Our hearts were made
To hold such gifts
All days throughout the year!

*The love of God is shed abroad
in our hearts. Rom. 5:5*

CONTENTS

Marjorie Ainsborough Decker

Marjorie Decker is a #1 National Bestseller author who is well-known and loved for her distinct story-telling style.

A native of Liverpool, England, Marjorie now resides in the United States with her husband, Dale. They are parents of four grown sons.

Her Christian Mother Goose® Classics have endeared the trust of parents and the twinkle of children around the world.

Along with authoring ten books in the Christian Mother Goose® Series, Marjorie brings fresh enthusiasm and dynamic teaching to sound, Biblical scholarship. There is a pleasant nostalgia to her children's books with a curious appeal to Bible lovers of all ages . . .

Recognized by the Christian Booksellers Association as one of the "Top Ten Bestselling Authors of The Decade", Mrs. Decker is also a frequent guest of national radio and television, a recording artist and popular Conference Speaker.